A BLUE
...IEN

Written by
KATE RUTTLE

Illustrated by
ELEFTHERIA-GARYFALLIA
THERI

First published in 2011
by Wayland

This paperback edition
published in 2012 by Wayland

Wayland
338 Euston Road
London NW1 3BH

Wayland Australia
Level 17/207 Kent Street
Sydney, NSW 2000

Series editor: Louise John
Designer: Paul Cherrill
Consultant: Kate Ruttle

A CIP catalogue record for this book is available
from the British Library.

ISBN 9780750266543

Printed in China

Wayland is a division of Hachette Children's Books,
an Hachette UK company. www.hachette.co.uk

All photos © Shutterstock, with the exception of the
swing and slide on page 16 and the net on page 18.

FIZZ WIZZ PHONICS is a series of fun and exciting books, especially designed to be used by children who have not yet started to read.

The books support the development of language, exploring key speaking and listening skills, as well as encouraging confidence in pre-reading skills.

LITTLE BLUE ALIEN is all about oral blending. Blending is an important skill that children need in order to begin to start reading. Blending happens when you see or hear a string of individual sounds and you **blend** (combine) them together to make a word. When doing blending activities with children, it is important to recognise the number of sounds and not the number of letters in the word, for example sh~ee~p has three sounds and not six.

This book encourages children to begin to hear the individual sounds in words. Throughout the book, Zog the alien speaks in sounds. When you read Zog's speech aloud with your child, say the sounds you can hear in the words, for example the sounds in 'spoon' are s~p~oo~n.

Try to read Zog's speech in an alien voice, and encourage your child to do the same. Children will enjoy learning that words are made up of sounds, and blending the sounds together.

For suggestions on how to use **LITTLE BLUE ALIEN** and for further activities, look at page 24 of this book.

Blend:
h~e~ll~o is **hello**
Z~o~g is **Zog**

Bump! A loud noise woke Yan up.
She crept downstairs and opened
the back door.

"H~e~ll~o," said a little blue alien.
"I am Z~o~g."

Blend:
b~ir~d is **bird**
c~a~t is **cat**
d~o~g is **dog**

Zog was visiting Earth to look
at lots of different things.
"What do you want to see?" asked Yan.

Zog showed Yan some photographs.
"B~ir~d, c~a~t, d~o~g!" he cried.

Blend:
c~u~p is **cup**
s~p~oo~n is **spoon**
b~ow~l is **bowl**

At breakfast time, Zog showed Yan
and Dad some more photographs.
"That's a cup, a spoon and a bowl!" said Yan.

8

Zog pointed to Dad's breakfast.
"C~u~p, s~p~oo~n, b~ow~l!" said Zog.

Blend:
s~c~ar~f is **scarf**
c~oa~t is **coat**
h~a~t is **hat**

After breakfast, Dad and Yan got ready to go out. It was a windy day so Yan put on her scarf, coat and hat.

Zog was excited and pointed to Yan.
"S~c~ar~f, c~oa~t, h~a~t!" he cried.

Blend:
c~ar is **car**
b~i~ke is **bike**
t~r~u~ck is **truck**

Then Zog, Yan and Dad went outside.
Zog wanted to see even more things.
"This is Dad's car," said Yan.

Zog, Yan and Dad drove down the street.
"C~ar, b~i~ke, t~r~u~ck!" shouted Zog.

Blend:
m~ea~t is **meat**
b~r~ea~d is **bread**
e~gg~s is **eggs**

At the supermarket, Zog was surprised to see all the food. The people were even more surprised to see an alien out shopping!

"What shall we look at first?" asked Dad.
"M~ea~t, b~r~ea~d, e~gg~s̩!" said Zog.

Blend:
d~u~ck~s is **ducks**
s~w~i~ng is **swing**
s~l~i~de is **slide**

After all the shopping, Dad took Yan and Zog to the park.
"Shall we feed the ducks?" asked Yan.

But Zog thought the slide was more fun!
"D~u~ck~s, s~w~i~ng, s~l~i~de!"
he yelled.

Blend:
f~i~sh is **fish**
ch~i~p~s is **chips**
c~a~ke is **cake**

When Ben went home, it was time for tea.
Zog showed Mum what he wanted to eat.
"Ok, let's have fish and chips!" said Mum.

For pudding, there was a chocolate cake.
"F~i~sh, ch~i~p~s, c~a~ke,"
laughed Zog.

Blend:
m~oo~n is **moon**
s~t~ar~s is **stars**
h~o~me is **home**

After tea, Zog was tired. He had
some last photographs to show.
"Is it time to go home, Zog?" asked Dad.

Yan was sad. She wanted Zog to stay.
"M~oo~n, s~t~ar~s, h~o~me,"
said Zog.

Further Activities

These activities can be used
when reading the book one-to-one,
or in the home.

These activities can be used when
using the book with more than one
child, or in an educational setting.

P4 • Talk about what might make sounds in the night in a house.
Walk round the house together, thinking about what makes
sounds. Listen to the sound of the fridge, a boiler, a cat flap.
What else might make sounds in your house?

P6 • Say the individual sounds in the words in the pink panel.
Can you then blend the sounds together to say the whole word?

P8 • When you say Zog's sounds on this page, point to the things
in the picture that he wants to see.
• Now go into your kitchen - can you find the same things?
Speak like Zog and just say the sounds, not the words.

P10 • Collect things that you wear outside, for example a coat, hat,
scarf, boots (b~oo~t~s), gloves (g~l~o~ve~s). Can you say the
whole word and put on the article of clothing?

P12 • Go for a walk, looking at what is around you through Zog's
eyes. What might he be excited to see?
• Try sounding out the words of the objects Zog might see outside,
and then blend the sounds to make a word, for example
t~r~ee / tree, g~r~a~ss / grass.

P14 • Look at items of food in your kitchen. Sound out words like Zog
does, then say the whole word, for example f~r~ui~t / fruit,
j~ui~ce / juice.

P16 • Do you ever go to the park to feed the ducks? What food might
you feed to the ducks? Can you say the whole word and the
individual sounds in the word, b~r~ea~d.

P18 • Before you read the words in the blue panel, can you name the
objects in Zog's photos? Now read the words in the blue blending
panel, saying the sounds first, followed by the whole word.

P20 • Look carefully at the food Zog is eating with the family.
Say the sounds in each word, then say the whole word.
For example p~ea~s / peas, w~a~t~er / water, ch~e~rr~ie~s /
cherries, ch~o~c~o~l~a~te / chocolate.

P22 • What do you know about space? Can you name things that Zog
might see on his way home? For example, p~l~a~n~e~t~s /
planets, c~o~m~e~t / comet, m~i~l~k~y w~ay / milky way.

P4 • Look together at the alien. How is he feeling?
How do you know?
• As a group ask each other what makes you feel
happy and excited? Can you guess why the alien
is happy and excited?

P6 • As you say Zog's sounds, can you point to each
photo of the things he wants to see?
• Talk about why he might have come to Earth.

P8 • Talk about what is the same and what is different about
Zog's photos and the cup, spoon and bowl that Dad is using.
• Point to each of the objects and sound them out, saying the
full word after you have said the sounds, for example c~u~p / c

P10 • Read the words in the green panel as a group.
What else might Yan need to wear on a windy day?

P12 • Find a book with a street scene in it. You could look at the stre
scene in Fizz Wizz Phonics: Sizzling Sausages, pages 8–9 and
10–11. Can you find a b~i~ke and a c~ar in this scene, too?
How about a m~a~n and a d~i~gg~er?

P14 • Use the Internet to find a picture of a shop. Sound out
words like Zog does saying the sounds then the whole word
each time, such as c~a~ke / cake, f~i~sh / fish.

P16 • Once you have read the text on this page, point to the things in
the picture. Can you say the sounds and then the whole word?
T~r~ee / tree, s~t~o~ne / stone, g~r~a~ss / grass,
s~k~y / sky, b~u~sh / bush.

P18 • As a group say the sounds in the blue panel, as you point to th
things in the picture. Then see if you can say the whole word.

P20 • What do you like to eat best? Can you draw your favourite foo
Can you say the individual sounds and then blend the sounds t
make the words of the items you have drawn?

P22 • Can you remember any of the things that Zog saw during his v
to Earth?